I Hate Poetry

Ella Williams

BookLeaf Publishing

Presentation by *BookLeaf Publishing*

Web: www.bookleafpub.com

E-mail: info@bookleafpub.com

ISBN: 9789357617246

First edition 2022

*This book is dedicated to Dragonfly,
Butterfly, Luna, all of my other guppies,
Cuddles, Bug-a-lug and Sunset.*

ACKNOWLEDGEMENT

I would like to acknowledge my Mummy and Daddy for supporting me during this writing challenge. I would also like to acknowledge my cats Lolly and Mason for being there for me too.

Ella Williams

PREFACE

Preface provided by Ella's mother.

"Every child is an artist. The problem is how to remain an artist once we grow up." - Pablo Picasso

To encourage our reluctant poet to write, we asked Ella to pick a new subject of interest on each day of the challenge. Ella was then asked many open-ended questions about the chosen subject and all of her responses were written down.

"How does it feel when...?"
"Why do you think that...is important?"
"What do you think would happen if...?"

After reading through her initial answers, Ella was asked even more questions, which helped to bring out her wonderful vocabulary and unique insights.

"Why does it make you feel that way?
"Can you explain what you mean by...?
"Can you describe this in a different way?"

Ella was then encouraged to shuffle her comments and thoughts into stanzas.

Some of the poems followed a structure, such as the introductory haiku "Day One", an attempt at a limerick "Sisterly Love" and the sonnet "In Our House". But for most of the poems Ella was never encouraged to follow any particular form. She was simply told that - poetry is art and art is whatever you decide.

Ella was predominately supported to write during the challenge by her mother, but on one occasion she was supported by her father. See if you can guess which poem resulted from this particular collaboration.

Day One

I don’t know the date.
Is today the day we start?
A haiku will do

What does it feel like to hold a tadpole?

Tadpoles are tickly,
Somersaulting inside of frog spawn,
New life underneath a tall tree.

The tree is dead,
But it is beautiful in a way,
A home for birds? Bees? I don't know.

In the hot sun,
I see a clever cockroach,
Drifting down the stream on a bark boat.

The sun makes me tired,
But in the coolness of night,
I see Saturn, I see the moon and Jupiter.

The flames of the campfire flicker,
like the wings of a Phoenix,
Grumbling frogs sound more like meditating
dogs.

A dusty smell makes me feel like I will sneeze,
But I never do.
It is nice to be in nature.

Unhappy Earthday

On the day I was born, I was wrapped in a blanket,
Protected from the chill of a rattling air conditioner.
Meanwhile, a global heat record was broken.

On my first birthday, thousands of walruses came ashore,
Crushing each other with nowhere else to rest.
The warm winters melted away all of the icebergs.

On my third birthday, Lucifer made Europe sweat.
The fountains ran dry and old people died.
Gelato dripped onto the pavement in Rome.

On my fifth birthday, the Amazon turned to ashes,
Farmers slashed and burned and the animals choked.
The men in charge said it was all a lie.

On my seventh birthday, we hid from a virus,
The human infection spread in every direction.
And I didn't bother planning a party.

A Disappearing Universe

Trapped in a box,
COVID made the walls close in.
Scared that the world will always be this small.
Will I ever go to the cinema again?
A worrier waiting for warriors to deliver the vaccine.
Who will test them?
The old? The young? Even babies?
What if it is deadly?
Doctors and nurses stuck in an endless loop.
The numbers going up, the numbers going down.
Someone's Mum, someone's Dad, someone's child,
Lost.

Sisterly Love

Today my brother turned three
So, I tried to sell him for free
He's noisy and rude
Likes to dance in the nude
And always following me.

Everything I know about chickens

My favourite chicken is called Ice cream.
She is kind and fluffy and sweet.
Although she lays a lot of eggs,
She's not the broodiest hen you'll meet.

Red chickens fade as they age,
Black chickens are silky and shine.
White chickens are very easily spooked,
Except the one that's mine.

Her pillowy rear is nice to hold,
And her pouflle is a delight.
It looks a bit like the brim of a hat,
And it shields her eyes from sight.

Oh, how I love my Ice cream,
And her eggs of turquoise and blue.
Please never let her know,
I'd like to eat some chicken too.

Things I learned on the internet

Men to the left, because women are always right.
Paper can cut anything when it is spinning fast enough.
You can forget that a friend has moved away, if you find them on Roblox.

Defying Gravity

With my head under the water,
I tap the side of the bath.
At first with my fist,
Bonk, bonk, bonk.
And then with my finger tips,
Tink, tink, tink.
I imagine the sound waves making ripples in the water.
They bounce off the smooth metal walls of the bath and enter my brain.
It must be different to how sound moves through the air.
Underwater the sound is clearer and I like how it echos,
The warm water wraps me in a soft blanket,
And folds me in a gentle hug.
It gives me superpowers and I can defy gravity.

The Bakery on O'Connell Street

At the bakery on O'Connell Street,
A neon sign says "24/7 Heaven".
My milkshake arrives,
It is bigger than my head.
I couldn't decide on chocolate or strawberry,
so the nice lady gave me both.

In my croissant, the edges of the ham are
slightly crispy.
The cheese oozes and there are too many layers
of pastry to count.
How do they always get it just right?

There is a guy here eating a ginormous
doughnut.
Nobody has ordered exactly the same thing,
But we will all experience a sugar crash later.

For dessert, a magnificent creation,
Containing exactly 209 layers and 2 and half
sticks of butter,
A ton of cinnamon sugar and the smallest pinch
of salt.
Sacrebleu! It tastes like "Bonjour!"

The chocolate must be French at the bakery on
O'Connell Street.

(Editor's note: This poem is not sponsored)

A Big Saddness

When the snowflakes fall slowly,
Each one is a prickle in my mind.
A big sadness is coming,
But I haven't yet figured out how to stop it.

When the snowflakes fall fast,
Thoughts in my head move like comets.
Being swallowed up by a black hole,
A big sadness buries me.

A big sadness is as heavy as a multiverse,
With one extra planet earth.
Weighing me down,
in blankets as dark as outermost space.

The coldness is unbearable.
Unbreakable.
My body feels frozen,
I can't even move my toes.

Every night I think about this,
And I pray to God.

Socks are itchy

If my feet could talk they would tell you that
socks are itchy.
Feet do not have hands to scratch,
They are feet.
How would you like it if somebody put a bag
over your head?
Socks are suffocating.
When my mum tells me to put my socks on, my
feet say
"Oh great, we are getting stuffed in the bags
again?! Stuff you!"

The Tree of Life

The tree of life is made of a hundred billion two
thousand and eight galaxies.
Moving, moving, moving, shifting, moving,
Purple, orange, green, brown, mellow yellow
and black.
Bigger than a thousand million moons,
It makes me feel happy, calm and safe.
Right now, we are in the leafy canopy,
But we will move deep down into the roots,
When the time is right.

Photoschnozmia

If you step into the sun,
And you really, really have to sneeze,
Because there is a tickle in your nose,
Please, sneeze into your elbow!
Don’t sneezed on the nice lady wearing fancy clothes,
And do a sassy walk away,
And pretended nothing happened.

This is what it is like to live with photoschnozmia.

(Editor's note: Photoschnozmia is better known as "photic sneeze reflex")

In Our Home

In our home, Mummy controls the junk food,
She hands it out as long as we are nice,
If not she threatens to feed us just rice,
So we do not mess with the junk food dude.

My Mum mostly has a fun attitude,
And she buys me treats no matter the price,
And spends time with me playing games with dice,
Cheering me up when I'm in a bad mood.

My Mum's ancestor hung out with a King,
A poet who invented the sonnet,
Her talent, maybe that's where she got it?
Writing with Mum is a wonderful thing!

I'm so lucky it makes me shout HOORAY!
Mummy adds brightness to every day.

Phantom Blue

What is your opinion of phantom blue?
I think it looks like the ocean,
Swimming in seaweed.
Or a better earth,
With enough water for every creature.

An Acrostic Poem

Friendly to all, he’s a really good guy.
Always there for me, especially when times are
tough.
Relishing every moment together, with respect.
Teaching me about life, love and all kinds of
things.
Ella’s Dad is the best.
Really, truly.

Mistakes

Remember that time when you tried to feed me,
my brother's breakfast?
And the time that you wore your pants
backwards?
Remember that time when you burned the
brisket?
And the all of times that you have got us lost?

Remember all the times that you lost your keys?
Your keys, your phone or your bag?
Remember that time that you taught me to
swear,
When we were chased by ducks, under attack?

Remember that time that you graduated,
And got your tudor bonnet stuck on your head?

Despite all these things there is still one mistake
that you have never made...
Remember that time that Daddy pea-ed on the
floor?

(Editor's note: This poem makes a lot more
sense to those who were present at the time.
Sorry, to those who were not.)

I'm really sick!

My nose has a rock block.
The goop is gross, sticky, slimey.
There is a fire in my throat,
And a volcano in my stomach.
My muscles are all floppy
I think I have something awful...
But HOORAY, no school today!

Trophies

Proud might feel good for a while,
but not if you have too much.
Earning a trophy that is a special thing,
But if you have too many, then none are really special.
Every person on Earth should get two trophies,
One when they are born,
Because surviving is an achievement.
And the second when they die,
And they get to see the people that they have missed,
This is an achievement to be proud of.

Dragonfly

His fur was so fluffy, silky and smooth.
His eyes, were a beautiful shade of blue… or
was it brown?
Don't write that down!
It means that I have forgotten Dragonfly, but I
haven't.
I think about him every day.

My heart is sad and happy.
The sadness is a lot.
Is it ok to feel as sad as a hurricane?
The happiness is remembering love at first at
sight.
Remembering our connection.

Sometimes you lose somebody you love,
And you can never get them back.
Every night you feel that they are right there
next to you,
You feel that you are about to cry.
If you don't have someone to talk to, you might
end up talking to objects.
A box, a chair or a picture.
But nothing really helps.

Perfect

If I did not write one last poem,
Then this book would not be perfect.
Oh, I wrote one, just like that,
One last poem, it's perfect!

www.ingramcontent.com/pod-product-compliance
Lightning Source LLC
Chambersburg PA
CBHW062205160726
48282CB00027B/1008
* 9 7 8 9 3 5 7 6 1 7 2 4 6 *